SCOTNOTES

Number 2

The Poetry
of Edwin Morgan

Geddes Thomson

Ass᠊ ᠊᠊᠊᠊ ᠊᠊ ᠊᠊᠊᠊᠊᠊᠊ ᠊᠊᠊᠊᠊ ᠊᠊᠊᠊ '986

Published by
Association for Scottish Literary Studies
c/o Department of Scottish History
9 University Gardens
University of Glasgow
Glasgow G12 8QH

www.asls.org.uk

First published 1986
Reprinted 2000, 2001, 2003, 2006

© Geddes Thomson

Y821 MOR
1715125

A CIP catalogue for this title is available from the British Library

ISBN: 0 948877 00 6
ISBN-13: 978 0 948877 00 1

The Association for Scottish Literary Studies
is in receipt of subsidy from the Scottish Arts Council

Printed by Ritchie (UK) Ltd, Kilmarnock

CONTENTS

EDITORS' FOREWORD

The *Scotnotes* booklets are a series of study guides to major Scottish writers and literary texts that are likely to be elements within literature courses. They are aimed at senior pupils in secondary schools and students in further education colleges and colleges of education. Each booklet in the series is written by a person who is not only an authority on the particular writer or text but also experienced in teaching at the relevant levels in schools or colleges. Furthermore, the editorial board, composed of members of the Schools and Further Education Committee of the Association for Scottish Literary Studies, considers the suitability of each booklet for the students in question.

For many years there has been a shortage of readily accessible critical notes for the general student of Scottish literature. *Scotnotes* has grown as a series to meet this need, and provides students with valuable aids to the understanding and appreciation of the key writers and major texts within the Scottish literary tradition.

Lorna Borrowman Smith
Ronald Renton

ACKNOWLEDGEMENTS

The author and publishers wish to thank Edwin Morgan for permission to print the following poems in their entirety: 'Astrodome', 'Glasgow 5 March 1971', 'Manifesto' and 'Siesta of a Hungarian Snake' from *Poems of Thirty Years* (Carcanet, 1982); 'Man of My Time' from *Rites of Passage* (Carcanet, 1976). Also poems 89 and 100 from the sequence, 'The New Divan', and 'Pilate at Fortingall' from *Sonnets from Scotland*.

INTRODUCTION

The Wide World

'I think of poetry partly as an instrument of exploration, like a spaceship, into new fields of feeling or experience and partly a special way of recording moments and events, taking the 'prose' of them, the grit of the facts of the case, as being in our age extremely important'.[1]

Edwin Morgan's own words immediately suggest the essential appeal of his work to young people and, indeed, to all readers. Here is a poet of the present and of the future rather than of the past. These words also indicate the wide range of his subject-matter, from the exploration of the new and unknown, to the simple recording of 'the facts of the case' and including almost everything in between. His is a poetry of man's exciting possibilities — computers, space-ships, meetings with strange alien beings from other planets; but it is also a poetry of the story in today's newspaper and the encounter with reality in a Glasgow street.

He is, therefore, a difficult poet to pin down. His work cannot be arranged into neat thematic categories because of its wide range. The categories suggested in this booklet are mere suggestions, no more, which may help towards an initial appreciation of his work. But a poet who in successive poems (in *The Second Life*) writes about Ernest Hemingway, Marilyn Monroe, Edith Piaf, the domes of St Sophia in Istanbul, a white rhinoceros, a wolf, an Aberdeen train and the opening of the Forth Road Bridge resists neat pigeon-holing.

A similar variety is obvious when we come to consider form and language. Morgan has produced work in all forms from traditional rhyming sonnets to daring experiments in concrete poetry. His use of language varies from Glasgow dialect to attempts to create the language of the Loch Ness monster or men from Mercury!

Tone and attitude are also extremely varied, from the tragic to the playful. Consider the sympathy and the final agonised exclamation of pity for a blind hunch-back that we find in the concluding lines of 'In the Snack-bar':

Wherever he could go it would be dark
and yet he must trust men.
Without embarrassment or shame
he must announce his most pitiful needs
in a public place. No one sees his face.
Does he know how frightening he is in his strangeness
under his mountainous coat, his hands like wet leaves
stuck to the half-white stick?
His life depends on many who would evade him.
But he cannot reckon up the chances,
having one thing to do,
to haul his blind hump through these rains of August.
Dear Christ, to be born for this!

In 'Letters of Mr Lonelyhearts', by contrast, we are enter-
tained by a hilarious parody of a newspaper problem page. Mr
Lonelyhearts is the pseudonym of the journalist who has to deal
with some bizarre complications. Occasionally he becomes exas-
perated:

Mr Lonelyhearts loosened his tie
with a great sigh, closed the marshmallows.
He took a turn about the room, spoke
sharply to his budgerigar, stared out
at nothing passing, came back
and with a last marshmallow grimly
settled to type. Dear Puzzled, it went,
Look, you got back your money, so
what's all the fuss? I've got broken hearts,
roofs collapsing, no month's rent, I've got
crazy wills, incest, grandmothers locked out —
and so I'm to lose sleep over a monkey?

.   .   .   .

The thunder broke, and Mr Lonelyhearts
seized a sheet like lightning. Dear Rosie,
he wrote, Kill him. For a man
who'd take a snake basket
on his honeymoon, divorce
is peanuts. Shoot him,
get yourself a night's sleep.

The sheer variety of theme, technique, language and tone in
Edwin Morgan's work should not frighten or inhibit us. We
should, on the contrary, welcome it. Here is God's plenty, the

wide world, for us to explore with the poet. The purpose of this booklet is to offer some signposts, to encourage the reader on the initial stages of the journey.

Biography

Edwin Morgan was born in Glasgow on the 27th of April, 1920. His father was a clerk with a firm of local scrap merchants. In his introduction to a selection of his poetry in the anthology, *Worlds* (Penguin Education, 1974), he tells us something about his early years. From the beginning he was fascinated both by 'the romance of adventure' and 'the romance of facts'; preoccupations which were later to appear prominently in his poetry. He started to write while still at school (at Rutherglen Academy and later Glasgow High School); long fantastic prose narratives influenced by Jules Verne, H.G. Wells and Edgar Rice Burroughs. Again, he was never to lose this early interest in the fantastic and in science fiction.

His horizons were further widened during the next few years by two key episodes in his life. The first of these was his enrolment at Glasgow University at the age of seventeen. There he studied for a degree in English and began, for the first time, to read modern poetry, not just in English, but in various European languages. This interest in foreign literature was later reflected in his wide-ranging translations.

The second key event was the interruption of his university career by the Second World War. Like so many young men of the time he had temporarily to abandon home and career to play his part in the defeat of Hitler's Germany. In Morgan's case he served in the Royal Army Medical Corps, mainly in the Middle East from 1940 to 1946. This first taste of travel overseas stirred a life-long interest. The colourful Middle Eastern world of his war service is re-created in the poem sequence, 'The New Divan', published in 1977. Morgan has since travelled widely in many European countries, including Hungary and Russia.

After war service he completed his English degree at Glasgow University, where he became a lecturer in 1947. He pursued his academic career at Glasgow until 1980 when he retired with the rank of Titular Professor of English.

Such a bald recital of the available facts of his life offers only very general pointers. Morgan has not published an autobiography and is not a poet who deals exclusively, or even very often, with his direct personal experience. For the real story, his life and work as a writer, we must go to the writing itself.

The Poetry

The first published poetry appeared in the 1950s with *The Vision of Cathkin Braes* (1952), but his first major collection was *The Second Life*, published by Edinburgh University Press in 1968. This volume exemplifies the wide range of his works, containing examples of poetry based on newspaper reports, poems with a Glasgow setting, love poetry, concrete poetry, and poems on science-fiction themes and autobiographical topics. The significantly named *From Glasgow to Saturn* (Carcanet, 1973), the second major collection, displays an even wider range of themes and techniques. A feature of this volume is the large number of poems in which a first person voice is assumed by Morgan in songs, monologues and dialogues. Four years later, a third important collection was published, *The New Divan* (Carcanet, 1977). This volume is dominated by the title-poem, 'The New Divan', a hundred-part sequence which shows the mature Morgan at his most accomplished. It is followed by 'Memories of Earth', a major science-fiction poem. The remainder of the volume is as varied as ever.

These three collections, plus other important work such as *Instamatic Poems* (Ian McKelvie, 1972) and various previously uncollected poems, are gathered in the major retrospective collection, *Poems of Thirty Years* (Carcanet, 1982), the most useful guide to Morgan's poetic achievement. His most recent publication, *Sonnets from Scotland* (Mariscat Press, 1984) shows Morgan using the strictly disciplined sonnet form to explore the condition of his native Scotland — past, present and future.

In addition to the collections mentioned above, the poetry of Edwin Morgan is readily accessible in a great number of anthologies. Most useful, because they contain an extended selection of his work along with introductions and notes, are *Twelve Modern Scottish Poets* edited by Charles King (U.L.P., 1971) and *Worlds* edited by Geoffrey Summerfield (Penguin Education, 1974). The latter volume is interesting in that the introduction, written by Morgan himself, provides some rare information about the poet's early life and writing experience.

Translations

Right from the start of his writing career, Edwin Morgan has been a prolific translator of poetry into English and Scots. He has translated from French, German, Italian, Spanish, Russian and Hungarian amongst other languages. The poets involved read like a roll of honour of modern European literature: Yevtushenko, Voznesensky, Pasternak and Mayakovsky from Russia; Montale and Quasimodo from Italy; Lorca from Spain; Brecht from Germany. Many of these translations are collected in *Rites of Passage* (Carcanet, 1976).

There is not space in this booklet for a detailed consideration of Morgan's translations, but their importance must be emphasised. They demonstrate, in the clearest possible way, Morgan's openness to influences from outside Scotland. A translator does two important things. First of all, he pays a compliment to the foreign writer whom he translates. The second thing is the translator's gift to his own countrymen. It is as if he says — 'Here is something worthwhile from a foreign culture, something we should know about and which I've tried to bring to you'.

Here is Morgan's translation of a poem by the modern Italian poet, Salvatore Quasimodo. It is called 'Uomo Del Mio Tempo' — 'Man of my Time':

> You are still the one with the stone and the sling,
> man of my time. You were there in the cockpit
> winged with hatred, dials set for death
> — I saw you — in the armoured car, at the gallows,
> at the torturer's wheel. I saw you! — it was you,
> devoting your exact science to destruction,
> without love, without Christ. You kill today
> as always, as your fathers killed, as the beasts
> that saw you for the first time also killed.
> And this blood smells as rank as in the day
> one brother said to another brother: 'Let us
> go to the fields'. And that cold, stubborn echo
> has penetrated now to you, to the bones of your life.
> Blot from your memory, O sons, the clouds of blood
> that mount and mount from the earth, forget your fathers:
> their tombs are sinking into the ashes, the wind
> and the dark birds cover over their hearts.[2]

Influences

Appropriately enough, in view of what we have already learned, many of the important literary influences on Morgan's work originate far from Scotland. In particular, certain North

American writers of the 1950s and 60s interested him. These were the Beat poets and the Black Mountain poets. 'Beat', a word of disputed origins, referred to the life style of these writers as well as their literary work. This consisted of an individualistic search for happiness and personal fulfilment and a vehement rejection of what they saw as modern America's worship of materialist values. Leading Beat poets included Allen Ginsburg, Gregory Corso and Lawrence Ferlinghetti. The Black Mountain poets were so-called because several of them taught at the liberal Black Mountain College in South Carolina, and published important work in the magazine 'Black Mountain Review' from 1954 to 1957. Among the leading Black Mountain poets were Charles Olsen, Robert Duncan and Robert Creeley.

Very generally, it would be fair to state that both these groups of writers scorned traditional restraints on the tone, subject-matter and form of poetry. For them the traditional poem with its subtle vocabulary, finely-tuned emotional expression, neat versification and lines of approximately equal length, lay inert and dead on the printed page, totally failing to communicate with a modern readership.

They advocated a more direct approach: poetry had to become a speaking voice to reach its potential audience. Not surprisingly, these poets often by-passed print in favour of poetry readings. They wrote mostly in unrhymed free verse with no restrictions on line-length, depending instead on rhythmic repetitions, exclamations and pauses (the rhythms of speech, in fact) to give shape to their work. On the printed page the typographical arrangement of words, phrases and lines was often very important. These poets addressed the reader of their subject directly. Their aims were always to convey an unharnessed emotional attitude towards their subject-matter and to jolt the reader into an emotional response, whether of shock, anger or amusement.

The result was poetry as direct as a megaphone and Morgan found it immensely liberating, although it should be pointed out that Morgan did not necessarily share the political or social programmes advocated by these writers. (For instance, he firmly rejected the back-to-nature communal living theories propounded by many of them).

What attracted Morgan to these writers was their open approach to poetry, their ideas of what poetry could be. But behind these writers lay the influence of the great nineteenth-century poet Walt Whitman, who, in turn, has been an obvious influence on Morgan. One further major influence from the USA was the work of the poet William Carlos Williams, whose long poem 'Paterson' gives an affectionate account of his home town in much the same way as Morgan has done for Glasgow in a series of shorter poems.

Morgan's translations provide a guide to the European influences on his work. What is noticeable is that many of the poets he has translated fall into one of two categories — poets of public commitment or poets notable for innovative or experimental work.

'Commitment', or the lack of it, is an issue that has been much discussed with regard to modern literature. Very roughly, the question raised is this: how far should the writer commit himself, use his work as a vehicle for his political or social opinions? There is an obvious danger in open commitment: the poet is in danger of becoming a platform speaker, a preacher even. Would it not be better, more truly poetical, to be a recorder, to describe and react as sensitively as possible, to let the poem, as it were, speak for itself'?

Morgan, in fact, does both as he sees fit. Sometimes he is the poet of commitment and very often, especially towards the end of a poem, he will make his own view plain or actually tell the reader what to do or how to react. Equally often, however, he is the poet as recorder carefully keeping out his own opinions, letting the content and the language he has chosen speak for themselves.

But from his admiration for writers such as Brecht and Mayakovsky, Morgan has formed a strong belief that poetry should 'speak out' much more than it does on all the issues that concern modern man.

> This lack of serious care, this process of glossing over and soften-ing, this lazy draping with a false timelessness, this distancing and dissolving of conflict — what are these but a fear of statement and commitment, a form of studied self-deprecation, a desperate dis-belief in the power of poetry to speak out on men and society?[3]

WHAT IS POETRY?

This booklet began with Edwin Morgan's own definition of poetry. Everyone has his or her own answer to the question — 'What is poetry?' Sometimes the answer is vague or simple and sometimes it is very precise and complicated. Sometimes it is followed by another equally challenging question — 'What is the use of poetry, anyway?' That seems, on the face of it, a relevant question, because poetry does not seem to have a use in the sense that a hammer has a use for knocking in nails. Many people seem to get along perfectly well in their daily lives without poetry. Yet how often, when watching a great footballer or an ice-skater, are we moved to murmur something about 'poetry in motion'? Which proves, perhaps, that most of us have a vague sense of poetry as the recognition of the beautiful in our lives. Yet, on a more basic level, another possible answer to the question 'What is poetry?' is that poetry consists of verses and stanzas and that it must rhyme. Young children often give this answer.

Both of these ideas — that poetry is the expression of the beautiful or that poetry rhymes — are rather simple and vague. It would be easy to find many poems which do not deal with 'the beautiful' and equally easy to prove that most modern poems do not rhyme. And yet these ideas have more than a grain of truth in them, because they fasten on two essential features of poetry. A successful poem, like a successful song or a successful painting, does appeal to our sense of the beautiful. We feel content, satisfied by the experience of the poem, by the sense that something significant has been well-expressed in words, just as we are left content and satisfied by the foot-baller's well-struck pass which leads to a goal or the ice-skater's precisely-executed figure. This is the case even when the poem deals with one of the less pleasant aspects of human life.

Equally, the requirement that poetry should be in verses and should rhyme, is not entirely naive, because it is a recognition that a successful poem must have a shape, a form, and must appeal to our ear as well as our intellect. Poetry is sound and form as well as sense and this is why it is impossible to reduce a successful poem to a prose equivalent without losing some essential aspects of the poem.

The best approach to poetry is to take each individual poem

on its own terms and make a judgement as to whether it satis-
fies us, recognizing that there are no unbreakable rules with
regard to subject-matter or form. This approach is particularly
important when studying the poetry of Edwin Morgan, because
we will find that he recognizes no limitations on subject or form.
Indeed he has often been criticised or ridiculed for challenging
the usual ideas that people have about poetry.

Here is one example of Morgan's challenging style:

> i am, horse
> unhorse, me
> i am, horse
> unhorse, me
> i am, horse
> unhorse, me
> i am horse:
> unhorse me!
> (From 'Centaur')

This is an example of concrete poetry. It is a type of poetry
which depends for its effect as much on the actual layout on
the page, as on any linear reading of the poem from beginning
to end. The poet seems to be saying 'Look at this!' rather than
expressing his own feelings about the subject. Many people find
this disturbing because it does not fit their idea of what poetry
should be. Yet when we examine 'Centaur' more closely, we are
forced to conclude that the poem is constructed out of meaningful words and that it conveys something to the reader by
means of the lay-out and punctuation as well as these words.
The centaur was a mythological being, half man, half horse. The
poem might be looked at as the thoughts of this divided being.
He is himself — 'me i am' — but he is both horse and man. The
poem's repetitions suggest his struggle to escape into a definite,
unambiguous identity and the final line with the exclamation
mark — 'unhorse me!' — is an agonised plea to be human.

However, in a concrete poem, the sound can take over
almost completely:

> oa! hoy! awe! ba! mey!

> *who saw?*

> rhu saw rum. garve saw smoo. nigg saw tain. lairg saw lagg.
> rigg saw eigg. largs saw haggs. tongue saw luss. mull saw yell.
> stoer saw strone. drem saw muck. gask saw noss. unst saw cults.
> echt saw banff. weem saw wick. trool saw twatt.

how far?

from largo to lunga from joppa to skibo from ratho to shona from
ulva to minto from tinto to tolsta from soutra to marsco from
braco to barra from alva to stobo from fogo to fada from gigha to
gogo from kelso to stroma from hirta to spango.

This is the beginning of a poem which Morgan called 'Canedolia,
An Off-Concrete Scotch Fantasia'. One can have as much fun
reciting it loudly and with spirit as Edwin Morgan obviously had
in creating it. It certainly is more than an ordinary alphabetical
gazetteer of Scottish place-names! Poetry, Morgan seems to be
saying in a poem like this, is often sheer delight in language itself, in the sounds we humans make, and delight also in the
arrangement of sounds and in playing games with language.
Sense, which is usually so important, should sometimes take a
back seat.

The chants and nursery rhymes of childhood confirm this:

Mrs White
Got a fright
In the middle of the night.
She saw a ghost
Easting toast
Half-way up a lamp-post!

We are not supposed to enquire too closely into the why and
wherefore of Mrs White's terrifying experience. The joy is in the
sound and in the nonsense of it all.

Morgan even carries the process a stage further by seeming
to move, occasionally, from word-sequences which appear illog-
ical and nonsensical into an apparent total meaninglessness:

— When did you start writing sound-poetry?

— Vindaberry am hookshma tintöl ensa ar'er.
  Vindashton hama haz temmi-bloozma töntek.

— I see. So you were really quite precocious.
  And did your parents encourage you?

— Zivva mimtod enna parahashtom ganna,
  spod zivva didtod quershpöt quindast volla!
  Mindetta brooshch quarva tönch bot.
  Spölva harabashtat su!
  (From 'Interview')

It would certainly be a mistake to take this too solemnly and seriously. That is the trap which Morgan lays for the over-respectful reader who thinks poetry should always be tremend-ously meaningful and significant. There is good fun here for the reader who hates pompous T.V. interviewers and can appreciate the ludicrous contrast.

These examples show us that we should approach Edwin Morgan's poetry without too many fixed ideas of what poetry should be. We should be prepared to read each poem with an open mind, responding to the experience of the poem itself.

WHAT ACTUALLY HAPPENS

'I am very strongly moved by the absolute force of what actually happens, because after all, that is it, there is really nothing else that has its poignance, its razor edge'.[4]

Thus Edwin Morgan, in an introduction to a selection of his work, gives us an important clue to his poetry. No other Scottish poet gives us such a consistent sense of a man who lives in our daily world of newspapers, television and films — the world of the mass media where a famine in Ethiopia, the launch of a satellite, the death of a pop-star and a sensational murder case are simultaneously reported to millions. He has made it clear in interviews that he finds it disappointing that so many modern poets have ignored this world of reportable reality which is the world of all of us whether we like it or not. Poets cannot, he claims, live in 'ivory towers' isolated from the world, taken up only by their personal concerns.

Equally, he rejects attempts to turn to the past, to a golden age before the complicated messy modern world. He once refused to compose an essay on how he started writing on the interesting grounds that nothing much that happened to him before the age of forty now interested him! It would be hard to find a clearer rejection of nostalgia.

Nor is he much interested in the idea that back to nature might be the cure for our modern ills. On the contrary he asserts — 'science is a cure for science, technology is a cure for technology'. We cannot go back — we must go forward.

The sheer consistency of his attitude is well-revealed when he writes about the massive redevelopment that has taken place in his native Glasgow over the last two decades: the demolition of the older tenements and road systems and their replacement by high-rise flats and ring roads. It is fashionable to criticise these new developments, to lament the passing of an older way of life based on a supposed close communal spirit engendered by tenement living. Morgan will have none of this. He sees the changes as necessary, indeed inevitable:

> . . . stalled lives never budge;
> They linger in the single-ends that use
> their spirit to the bone, and when they trudge
> from closemouth to laundrette their steady shoes
> carry a world that weighs us like a judge.
> ('Glasgow Sonnet x')

The new concrete Glasgow emerging from the rubble of the nineteenth century has a beauty of its own:

> Meanwhile the flyovers breed loops of light
> in curves that would have ravished tragic Toshy —
> clean and unpompous, nothing wishy-washy.
> Vistas swim out from the bulldozer's bite ...
> ('Glasgow Sonnet viii')

The reference is to Charles Rennie Mackintosh (1868-1928), by common consent Glasgow's greatest architect, many of whose buildings have, ironically, come under threat during the city's redevelopment.

Morgan's targets are those who want to preserve the past at all costs. They may be well-intentioned, but their ultimate effect is simply to 'prop-up' the past rather than preserve it in any meaningful way:

> Environmentalists, ecologists
> and conservationists are fine no doubt.
> Pedestrianization will come out
> fighting, riverside walks march off the lists,
> pigeons and starlings be somnambulists
> in far-off suburbs, the sandblaster's grout
> multipy pink piebald facades to pout
> at sticky-fingered mock-Venetianists.
> Prop up's the motto. Splint the dying age.
> Never displease the watchers from the grave.
> ('Glasgow Sonnet vii')

So, we find in Morgan a rejection of the past for the past's sake and, in equal measure, a commitment to the present, to our 'global village' as it has been called.

Morgan's commitment to the present, to the world of reportable reality, is most evident in the poems of his first major collection, *The Second Life*, published in 1968 and in *Instamatic Poems* which appeared four years later.

The first three poems in *The Second Life* are occasioned by the deaths of three legendary figures of the modern age — the writer Ernest Hemingway; the film star, Marilyn Monroe; and the French singer, Edith Piaf. All three died in tragic circumstances: Hemingway was a suicide, while Marilyn Monroe and Edith Piaf both died of drug over-doses.

This is the spectacular world of screaming headlines, sensational revelations, stories that go round the world in twenty-four hours. We can all remember such events and, quite often, our reactions to them. Most people over thirty-five can actually remember where they were and what they were doing when they heard the news of President Kennedy's assassination in 1963. The deaths of Elvis Presley and John Lennon are more recent examples. Morgan's continued interest in the theme of the deaths of the famous is demonstrated by the much later poem 'A Good Year For Death' which deals with Presley amongst others.

Other poems in *The Second Life* deal with a less sensational reality. 'The Opening of the Forth Road Bridge', for example, responds to an event of Scottish rather than international significance, while the group of poems about Glasgow (which will be discussed elsewhere) is firmly located in a West of Scotland reality. Two of these Glasgow poems, 'King Billy' and 'The Starlings in George Square', again have their origins in newspaper stories. The former deals with the spectacular funeral of Billy Fullerton, a former Protestant gang leader during Glasgow's hungry and violent nineteen-thirties, which was widely reported in the local press. The latter is a humourous treatment of the local media controversy about how to deal with the plague of starlings whoch were defacing the city's municipal buildings during the nineteen-sixties. The other Glasgow poems in *The Second Life* deal with actuality at a personal level; the poet's encounters with people in the streets of the city — young people, a heart attack victim, a drunk man, a blind hunch-back.

In almost all of the poems based on reportable reality the newspaper reports which gave rise to the poems are taken as read, as it were. Morgan may use significant details from the reports, but rather than re-reporting the event he adopts one or more of several typical approaches. Sometimes, for example, he concentrates on his own reactions to the event. Alternatively, he sometimes recreates the event entirely, through the use of symbolism or by attempting to create the subjective reality of the person involved. Examples will make these difficult points clearer.

'The Death of Marilyn Monroe' contains the actual reported details of the tragedy in phrases such as 'nembutal bed' and lines such as 'They had to lift her hand from the bedside telephone'. But the main thrust of the poem is Morgan's attempt to convey his own reaction to the tragedy, which is that Marilyn Monroe was essentially a victim of the pressures of the Hollywood star system. This he does by using a very direct series of

questions and exclamations, reminiscent of the technique of the
Beat poets:

> What innocence? Whose guilt? What eyes? Whose breast?
> Crumpled orphan, nembutal bed,
> white hearse, Los Angeles,
> DiMaggio! Los Angeles! Miller! Los Angeles! America!
>
> .   .   .   .
>
> Los Angeles! Olivier! Los Angeles! Others die
> and yet by this death we are a little shaken, we feel it,
> America.

This very public style, including the use of 'we', the first person
plural, is appropriate to the pathetically public nature of the
death and, of course, of the life. The larger-than-life Hollywood
hysteria of the event is also being conveyed. Finally, Morgan's
tone is accusatory: he is almost the public prosecutor putting
Hollywood in the dock and, again, the style is an appropriate
vehicle to convey this:

> And if she was not responsible, not wholly responsible, Los Angeles?
> Los Angeles? Will it follow you around? Will the slow
> white hearse of the child of America follow you around?

'The Old Man and the Sea , which deals with the suicide of
the great American writer Ernest Hemingway, employs symbolism to express Morgan's sense of the 'questions not answers'
which 'chill the heart'. The title of the poem refers to one of
Hemingway's most famous books in which an old fisherman
struggles in vain to bring a great fish to land. For Morgan, Hemingway is the old man of the writer's own creation, an appropriate identification because Hemingway tried to merge life and
art in a way that few writers have ever done.

The boxers, bull-fighters and big game hunters of Hemingway's fiction reflect his own real-life activities. When he could
no longer pursue these activities, either in art or in life, because
of failing creative and physical powers, his existence became in-
creasingly pointless.

Morgan uses one major symbol throughout the poem — a
cold white sea mist which drifts across the American continent
from the western sea-board until it reaches the writer in his
rural retreat. This white mist from the sea is an obvious symbol
of death:

And above the still lakes of Oregon
and the Blue Mountains into Idaho
eastward, white wings brushing the forests,
a white finger probing the canyon
by Wood River, delicate, persistent, at last
finding by the half-light, in a house of stone,
a white-bearded man like an old sea-captain
cleaning a gun. — Keep back the sea,
keep back the sea! No reassurance
in that daybreak with no sun,
his blood thin, flesh patched and scarred,
eyes grown weary of hunting
and the great game all uncaught.
It was too late to fight the sea.

In addition to the use of symbolism, the poem is notable also
for its form and its style. It consists of one very long unbroken
verse paragrpah, evidently intended to suggest the inevitability
of the chilling sea mist's progress towards the great writer. The
first sentence, in particular, stretches for no fewer than nineteen
lines and creates a sense of flowing power. Here is just a part of
the sentence, the opening lines:

And a white mist rolled out of the Pacific
and crept over the sand, stirring nothing —
cold, cold as nothing is cold
on those living highways, moved in
over the early morning trucks,
chilling the drivers in their cabins . . .

Stylistically, we can note the frequent repetitions, especially of
the word 'and', which is used almost biblically as in the opening
two lines quoted above. Again, the inevitability of the mist's
progress and the writer's death is powerfully suggested by this
use of repetition. Key elements in the poem are stressed by
clusters such as 'cold, cold as nothing is cold' and 'White wings
brushing the forests, / a white finger probing the canyon'. It is
surely no coincidence that repetition, especially of the word
'and', is a key element in Ernest Hemingway's own very recog-
nisable style.

'Je ne regrette rien', written in memory of Edith Piaf, re-
sembles 'The Old Man and the Sea' in that once again life and
art are identified. The title refers to her most famous song
which came to represent to the public the singer's attitude to
life. The technique however, is quite different. Morgan uses the

singer's own words to create her legendary life which was a triumph of spirit against adversity. First of all, the privations:

> But who counts years?
> Count the years I was blind?
> Dandled in a brothel? Taught by whores?
> Count the prayers that gave me my sight at Lisieux?
> Or the heartbeats of my daughter, in thousands,
> when I bore her at fourteen
> till she starved and died?
> Count the crusts I've had, or those I've given?

But the poem ends with the triumph of love which begins again with no regrets:

> We sway in the rain,
> He crushes my mouth.
> What could I regret
> if a hundred times
> of parting struck me
> like lightning if this
> lightning of love
> can strike and
> strike
> again!

Thus far we have seen Morgan recreating reportable reality in a variety of ways, but he has also been interested in a more objective approach, the poet as recorder of reality, rather than recreator of that reality.

This second option — the poet as recorder — occurs most obviously in a sequence called *Instamatic Poems* published in 1972. These poems are derived from newspaper reports or photographs which attracted Morgan's attention. The aim, as the term 'instamatic' suggests, is to record events in an almost photographic manner as they occur, as a press photographer might record them; to give the reader the sense that this is happening before his very eyes.

A typical instamatic poem is 'Glasgow 5 March 1971':

> With a ragged diamond
> of shattered plate-glass
> a young man and his girl
> are falling backwards into a shop-window.
> The young man's face
> is bristling with fragments of glass

and the girl's leg has caught
on the broken window
and spurts arterial blood
over her wet-look white coat.
Their arms are starfished out
braced for impact,
their faces show surprise, shock
and the beginning of pain.
The two youths who have pushed them
are about to complete the operation
reaching into the window
to loot what they can smartly.
Their faces show no expression.
It is a sharp clear night
in Sauchiehall Street.
In the background two drivers
keep their eyes on the road.

Here we see the poet as recorder par excellence. The whole effect depends on the contrast between the violent and shocking incident and the dead-pan way in which it is recorded. The present tense is used throughout to give immediacy. There is no discernible rhyme, rhythm or versification; nothing overtly poetical in the treatment. The poem consists of seven sentences which are, to all intents and purposes, straightforward statements of fact. The very title, 'Glasgow 5 March 1971', sounds like the prosaic note of time and place we might scrawl on the back of a holiday snap-shot which wasn't quite good enough to be stuck in the album.

Yet the subject-matter seems to call aloud for comment and reaction, rather than a cool, objective narration of the facts. The callousness of the two youths, who have dehumanised the young couple, used them almost as human bricks to carry out their smash and grab — this shocks and disgusts us. The plight of the lovers arouses our pity, while we cannot help wondering about the two drivers who 'keep their eyes on the road'. Surely they have seen and heard the incident. We wonder also about the society in which we live, where such things can happen and be ignored.

Such reactions suggest that Morgan has gained a more powerful effect by his dead-pan technique than he would have achieved by spelling out the 'message' to the reader at the end of the poem. In fact, a re-reading of the poem shows that the final effect is carefully calculated both in terms of structure and word-choice: the reader's reactions follow inevitably from the poet's technique.

The poem is in three parts, corresponding to the three couples involved. The first part describes the young couple falling helplessly through the plate-glass window. Images of sharpness are used to convey the horror — 'ragged diamond', 'bristling with fragments', 'broken window'. The most vivid image is that of the girl's leg which 'spurts arterial blood / over her wet-look white coat'.

The couple's emotions of 'surprise', 'shock' and 'pain' contrast with the two youths whose 'faces show no expression' in the second section. To them this is simply an 'operation'. Notice how the word 'smartly' is postponed to the end of the sentence to convey their heartless priorities of speed and efficiency. In the final section the 'camera' moves away to show us the two drivers who in the final line 'keep their eyes on the road'. That final line contains a powerful irony, because we realize that they keep their eyes on the road to avoid involvement, not because they are obeying the highway code. The young couple are caught between the callous indifference of the youths and the callous indifference of the car drivers. We are forced to reflect on which is worse. Is the second, perhaps, the cause of the first?

Irony, a rather 'sick' irony, is employed throughout the poem, presumably to convey the sense of a sick society. Consider 'the diamond of shattered plate-glass' which might be an ironic reference to the possibility that the young people were looking at diamond engagement rings just before their ordeal, or the real arterial blood on the girl's 'wet-look' white coat. Similarly, the youths' 'operation' might remind us of the clinical sharpness of a surgical operation.

This irony is most obvious in the lines 'It is a sharp clear night / in Sauchiehall Street'. 'Sharp', on the surface, might just refer to temperature (i.e., it was a cold night) but in its context it refers powerfully back to the cut and bleeding victims.

Examination of the instamatic poems as a whole reveals that certain features recur. Technique has already been discussed — the use of the present tense and an objective vocabulary. But we can also discern a typical subject matter. The incidents described tend to be dramatic, violent, bizarre — often shocking. As in the poem already analysed, Morgan's exclusion of emotional overtones usually has the paradoxical effect of making the poems extremely powerful. Reader response is created by cunning use of structure. Interesting instamatic poems include 'Translunar Space March 1972', 'Campobasso Italy', 'Venice April 1971', and 'Glasgow November 1971'. The latter poem is particularly worth analysis in terms of structure. It offers an interesting comparison with 'Glasgow 5 March 1971'.

Poems in which Morgan responds imaginatively rather than objectively to the world of reportable reality include 'A Good Year For Death', 'Iran', 'Che' and 'Resurrections'. 'Iran' deals with the punishment of an adultress in modern Iran and it is illuminating to compare this poem with 'The Death of Marilyn Monroe'. Similarly, 'Resurrections , which is a response to the death of the great Chinese leader, Chou En-lai, in 1976, is reminiscent in technique of 'Je ne regrette rien'. 'Che', about the death of Che Guevara, a revolutionary hero of the Cuban guerilla war, employs symbolism in the manner of 'The Old Man and the Sea'.

GLASGOW

Morgan's poems about his native city of Glasgow have been among his most popular. This is natural enough because most of them are relatively straightforward compared with, say, the science fiction work or the experiments with concrete poetry. They deal with the humorous, dramatic and often violent reality of a great post-industrial city and they have an immediate appeal to readers.

Yet it is important to place the Glasgow poems in the wider context of his work as a whole. Both the science fiction poems and the concrete experiments, for example, outnumber poems about Glasgow fairly comfortably and no-one can appreciate Morgan properly through an acquaintance with just the Glasgow poems. It is also important to realize that the placing of poems into categories by content or technique is essentially artificial. Morgan is always a Glasgow poet whatever his immediate subject-matter and, at the same time, always more than a Glasgow poet.

A good way of looking at most of the Glasgow poems is to see them as poems about street life. The streets are real Glasgow streets and they are named:

> Two girls running,
> running laughing,
> laughing lugging
> two rolls of linoleum
> along London Road —
> ('Linoleum Chocolate')

> Three o'clock. The bus lurches
> round into the sun. 'D's this go — ?'
> he flops beside me — 'right along Bath Street?'
> ('Good Friday')

> Clammy midnight, moonless mist.
> A cigarette glows and fades on a cough.
> Meth-men mutter on benches,
> pawed by river fog. Monteith Row
> sweats coldly, crumbles, dies
> slowly.
> ('Glasgow Green')

> Coming up Buchanan Street, quickly, on a sharp winter evening
> ('Trio')

These are the opening lines of four of the Glasgow poems; the
scene is exactly set in terms of time, place, even weather, but
especially in the naming of the actual street. Other poems reflect this exactitude in their titles 'Death in Duke Street', 'The
Starlings in George Square', 'At Central Station', 'Stobhill'. It is
as if the poet is saying, 'This is real. This actually happened.'
  In 'Glasgow Green' we find this point hammered home:

> This is not the delicate nightmare
> you carry to the point of fear
> and wake from, it is life, the sweat
> is real, the wrestling under a bush
> is real, the dirty starless river
> is the real Clyde . . .
>   ('Glasgow Green')

Real . . . But not just depressingly real. Often, the street scenes
are happy. People, especially young people, are caught up in a
sheer spirit of happiness which Morgan makes it his main busi-
ness to convey.
  In 'Trio', for example, he describes three young people
hurrying up Glasgow's Buchanan Street on a cold winter evening
at Christmas time. The poem begins prosaically enough, sketch-
ing in the main elements of the scene in the first five lines, but
then the lines expand in a welter of adjectives and exclamation
marks from lines 6 to 12 to suggest the 'cloud of happiness' and
the sense of well-being which the young people create and the
poet's reactions:

> The chihuahua has a tiny Royal Stewart tartan coat like a teapot-holder,
> the baby in its white shawl is all bright eyes and mouth like favours
>   in a fresh sweet cake,
> the guitar swells out under its milky plastic cover, tied at the neck
>   with silver tinsel tape and a brisk sprig of mistletoe.
> Orphean sprig! Melting baby! Warm chihuahua!

Morgan then makes his crucial point, which is an unconven-
tional one — that the happiness of this commercial Christmas of
presents carried home under coloured lights in a busy shopping
street is enough justification in itself without reference to Christ-
ianity:

> The vale of tears is powerless before you.
> Whether Christ is born, or not born, you
> put paid to fate, it abdicates
> > under the Christmas lights.
>
> Monsters of the year
> go blank, are scattered back,
> can't bear this march of three.

Morgan uses the device, probably learned from the American Black Mountain poets, of making the typographical lay-out of the poem reflect the sense, in:

> it abdicates
> > under the Christmas lights.

There are similar devices in the other Glasgow poems of this period, such as 'Good Friday' and 'Glasgow Green'.

'Trio , although it is in a way a repudiation of the central importance of the Christian message, does contain Christian elements which add a gentle irony to the poem. For example, the three young people are reminiscent of the Wise Men, the Magi, carrying gifts; the girl with the very young baby reminds us of Mary and the baby Jesus; the Christmas lights above make us think of the starry sky above Bethlehem. But for Morgan these Christian elements are almost incidental; the real point is still the sheer human happiness that the young people emanate:

> in their arms they wind
> the life of men and beasts, and music,
> laughter ringing them round like a guard

'Linoleum Chocolate' and 'To Joan Eardley' also celebrate the energy and spirit of ordinary Glasgow people, but it is particularly interesting to examine another Glasgow poem, 'Good Friday', and to compare it with 'Trio'.

Morgan, of course, does not ignore the darker aspects of life in his native city. A group of powerful poems depicts the violence and squalor to be found. Once again these are poems of the streets, the real 'mean streets' of Glasgow, which are named for us as if to emphasize their reality. Even the harshnesses of the Glasgow climate are precisely described — the grey clouds piling up over Riddrie in 'King Billy', the 'clammy midnight' of 'Glasgow Green', the 'sluggish winds' of 'Saturday night'. No details of degradation are spared in these poems. In 'Glasgow Green' a homosexual rape in a dark city park is vividly evoked through the words of the rapist. In 'Death in Duke Street' a

derelict man dies on a city pavement — 'a huddle on the greasy
street'. In 'At Central Station' a woman urinates in public, 'in
the middle of the day'.

Such uncompromising reality would be merely shocking,
disgusting and repulsive if Morgan contented himself with re-
portage or description — hellish messages from mean streets —
but Morgan's controlled compassion for those involved redeems
the material from bleak pessimism. He never forgets that these
outcasts and derelicts are entitled to at least some shreds of
human dignity.

'Glasgow Green', which deals with the down-and-outs who
haunt one of the city's largest public parks, is a good example
of Morgan's compassion. His technique in this poem is to use
an intricate imagery of water and liquid. For example, the scene
is set with 'clammy midnight' and 'Monteith Row sweats coldly'.
The outcasts 'sweat' in the darkness beside the 'diry starless
river'. A contrast is then drawn between the detergent-clean
washing that the women hang in the park by day and:

> the real Clyde, with a dishrag dawn
> it rinses the horror of the night
> but cannot make them clean

The poet then develops the symbolism of the liquid imagery
further with:

> The thorn in the flesh!
> Providence, water it!
> Do you think it is not watered?
>
> .   .   .   .
>
> Water the wildernes, walk there, reclaim it!
> Reclaim, regain, renew! Fill the barns and the vats!

We see that the original references to sweat and the dirty polluted
Clyde, suggesting a horror and guilt that can never be cleansed,
have been transmuted to a powerful plea for the life-giving
properties of water; water as the symbol of fertility. There is
even a reference to the biblical miracle of water changed into
wine

> Longing,
>   longing
>   shall find its wine.

In the last eight lines of the poem this water imagery is carried to its conclusion. The married women, sitting rocking their prams amidst the sanitised washing in the bright daylight, are seen as the lucky ones, almost complacent, because:

> the beds of married love
> are islands in a sea of desire.
> Its waves break here, in this park,
> splashing the flesh as it trembles
> like driftwood through the dark.

We realize that Morgan is conveying through his imagery that 'the sea of desire', however sordid, is the essential human condition; that the derelicts wrestling in the darkness beside the park benches are a part of that human condition.

Other poems which depict the darker side of Glasgow life are 'In the Snackbar', 'Death in Duke Street' and 'At Central Station'. It is interesting to compare them, in terms of subject-matter, technique and Morgan's attitude, with another particularly interesting poem in this group, 'King Billy'. As previously indicated, the poem was prompted by newspaper reports of the spectacular and incongruous funeral accorded to Billy Fullerton, who had been a prominent Protestant gang-leader in the city during the nineteen-thirties. That was a violent decade in Glasgow's history, a time when mass unemployment and poverty spawned dangerous frustrations. The Glasgow gangster and his favoured weapon, the open razor, became almost as notorious as the Chicago mobster and his sub-machinegun. Rival gangs were formed on territorial and sometimes religious lines. Violent clashes were frequent. Fullerton was the leader of the Bridgeton Billy Boys, a Protestant gang which maintained a bitter rivalry with a neighbouring Catholic gang, the Norman Conks, so called because they were based on Norman Street where many Catholics lived. There is an obvious pun inherent in this gang's name — Norman Conquerors — i.e., victors over King William and his followers.

The pitched street battles between the two factions — involving the use of razors, hatchets and sharpened bicycle chains — became such a serious social problem that in 1931 Percy Sillitoe, who had gained a reputation as a destroyer of gangs in Sheffield, was appointed Chief Constable of Glasgow; his remit — to destroy the 'razor gangs'. During the next few years gang-leaders were given heavy prison sentences. Sillitoe, as Morgan writes in the poem, 'scuffed the razors down the stank', i.e. pushed them down the drain.

This social history is integral to the poem in fact, 'King Billy' is a poem about social history and its shadowy parallel -- folk history or legend. It is not, despite the ironical title and the elaborate Protestant trappings of Fullerton's funeral, a poem about religious divisions and Glasgow's traditional sterile clash between the Orange and the Green. When Morgan, in the concluding lines, urges us to:

> Deplore what is to be deplored
> and then find out the rest

he is telling us to look beneath the violence and the religious bigotry to find the hard social circumstances which caused them.

Long before Fullerton died in the early nineteen-sixties, he had relapsed into obscurity, but enough of folk memory remained for his death to be marked. He was still a 'folk hero'. Morgan, in his poem, structured in three free-verse paragraphs, works out the contrasts and tensions between the violence of the past and its irrelevance in the present, between the glamour of the funeral and the deserted grave, between legend and reality.

The first verse exhibits a documentary film technique. The camera tilts slowly downwards from the clouds, 'grey over Riddrie', to the trees, the cemetery gates which gleam in the rain and the lamplight, to the 'huddled' gravestones, and finally zooms in to pick out a wreath — 'To Our Leader of Thirty Years Ago . The rest of the poem will explain what lies behind this sombre and desolate scene.

The rhythms of Morgan's free-verse technique are integrated with meaning and nowhere is this more apparent than in the second paragraph. It begins slowly, evoking the movement of Fullerton's funeral through the Glasgow streets. 'Bareheaded' and 'seriously', placed at the beginnings of lines, impede the flow of words, suggesting the hesitant rhythm of a dead march:

> Bareheaded, in dark suits, with flutes
> and drums, they brought him here, in procession
> seriously, King Billy of Brigton, dead,
> from Bridgeton Cross.

Then, with the phrase 'a memory of violence' the poem moves into the past:

> brooding days of empty bellies,
> billiard smoke and a sour pint.

The simmering discontent created by hunger, boredom and

unemployment is well suggested by the use of the plosives 'b' and 'p'; a discontent which boils over into violence:

> boots or fists, famous sherrickings,
> the word, the scuffle, the flash, the shout.

The movement now is quick; the violence sudden, full of purpose, deadly. But within a few lines the ultimate uselessness and sterility of it all is evident with:

> get
> the Conks next time, the Conks ambush
> the Billy Boys, the Billy Boys the Conks till
> Sillitoe scuffs the razors down the stank —

This last line, with the indeterminate dash at the end, 'quietens' the poem down, just as Sillitoe 'quietened' Glasgow's hard men, and the next few lines review Fullerton's life, his brief glory as a gang-leader and his decline to:

> a quiet man at last, dying
> alone in Bridgeton in a box bed.

Then Morgan, working out contrasts, as he does throughout, returns to the noise and movement of the huge funeral procession at which a thousand people stopped the traffic in memory of 'a folk hero' marching to the traditional strains of a flute band. He is careful to point out the seriousness and dignity of the occasion:

> the flutes
> threw 'Onward Christian Soldiers' to the winds
> from unironic lips, the mourners kept
> in step, and there were some who wept.

This stress on the procession's dignity is at the heart of Morgan's ultimate reaction. There is inherent irony in the poem's title and in the mourners' celebration of a violent and worthless life, but Morgan is evidently more interested and impressed by the spontaneous expression of communal memory which the funeral represents:

> it isn't the violence they remember
> but the legend of a violent man.

And so, in the final verse, which again uses contrast by stressing the silent aftermath of the funeral, we are told to:

> Deplore what is to be deplored
> and then find out the rest.

LOVE

Love is one of poetry's enduring themes. The experience of love is, after all, the nearest most people get to complete happiness and fulfilment.

Morgan's love poems stand rather apart from the rest of his work. They give us glimpses of private life and domesticity which are notably absent elsewhere: a flat with a balcony, a record collection, meetings in cafés, partings in bus-shelters, cigarettes burning in ash-trays, picnics, a trip to Glen Fruin, a party which breaks up in confusion and recriminations. However, these are glimpses only, because in other ways these are intensely private poems. The loved ones are never named or described in any detail, but always referred to simply as 'you' or 'your' with no indication of status. Curiously, this vagueness does not detract from the effectiveness of the poetry. It seems, instead, to give it a universal quality.

Both *The Second Life* and *From Glasgow to Saturn* contain a sequence of love poems. 'Sequence' is the appropriate word because in both volumes the love poems are printed one after the other. It is, moreover, obvious that each set of poems deals with a particular relationship. In *The Second Life* the relevant poems, in order, are 'The Unspoken', 'From a City Balcony', 'When You Go', 'Strawberries', 'The Witness', 'One Cigarette', 'The Picnic', 'Absence and 'Without It'. In *From Glasgow to Saturn* the sequence consists of 'Drift', 'Fado', 'After the Party', 'At the Television Set', 'From the North', 'The Milk-cart', 'Estranged' and 'For Bonfires'. *The New Divan* also contains a short group, again obviously charting a particular relationship — 'The Divide', 'Smoke', 'The Beginning' and 'The Planets'.

The sequences identified above deal with the joys of love, the moments of happiness and exaltation; but they also depict the agonies of love, the temporary nature of most relationships. It is strongly recommended that they be read as sequences rather than as individual poems, because then the unfolding drama of the personal relationship between two people will be better appreciated.

We have already seen the importance of imagery in poetry, particularly of a related set of images which ideally come to symbolize a poem's deepest layer of meaning. The water imagery in 'Glasgow Green' is a good example. Another reason for

reading Morgan's love-poetry in sequences is that it becomes
easier to realize that certain clusters of images recur in these
poems and that they are used symbolically.

The first such cluster relates to the physical aspect of love,
to the sense of touch. Lovers touch continually. They seek
union with one another. But physical union can only be temporary. Time brings inevitable separation. Morgan evokes the
happiness and sadness of this truth over and over again in his
love-poetry in references to lips, arms and, above all, hands that
touch:

But Glasgow days and grey weathers, when the rain
beat on the bus shelter and you leaned slightly against me, and the
    back of your hand touched my hand in the shadows, and
    nothing was said,
when your hair grazed mine accidentally as we talked in a cafe,
    yet not quite accidentally,
when I stole a glance at your face as we stood in a doorway and found
    I was afraid
of what might happen if I should never see it again.
    ('The Unspoken')

But in the dream I woke from, you
came running through the traffic, tugging me, clinging
to my elbow, your eyes spoke
what I could not grasp —
Nothing, if you were here!
    ('Absence')

Take care if you turn now to face me.
For even in this room we are moving out through stars
and forms that never let us back, your hand
lying lightly on my thigh and my hand on your shoulder
are transfixed only there, not here.

What can you bear that would last
like a rock through cancer and white hair?
('At the Television Set')

Where are you in this darkness? I put out
a hand, the branch outside
touches only old October air
and loses leaves, it is hard

>   to wish for you, harder to sleep, useless to weep.
>   How can I bear the darkness empty
>   and how can the darkness bear love?
>   ('The Milk-cart')

There are many other references in these poems to the longing
to touch, the physical nature of love.

Another recurring theme is the deep trust between lovers.
This is usually evoked by Morgan through images of relaxation,
particularly of sleep. The sleep of lovers after physical and spirit-
ual union is as relaxed, satisfying and innocent as the sleep of
children. The sleep of one lover, observed by the other, symbol-
ises childlike trust and utter openness, and inspires feelings of
tenderness and protectiveness in the lover who observes. But
here again, sleep implies its opposite — waking up. Sometimes
alone.

>   When you go,
>   if you go,
>   and I should want to die,
>   there's nothing I'd be saved by
>   more than the time
>   you fell asleep in my arms
>   in a trust so gentle ...
>   ('When You Go')

>   and I bent towards you
>   sweet in that air
>   in my arms
>   abandoned like a child ...
>   ('Strawberries')

>   I bore the darkness lying still, thinking
>   you were against my heart
>   ('The Milk-cart')

One of the most striking images in Morgan's love-poetry
occurs in the first line of 'One Cigarette':

>   No smoke without you, my fire.

The flame of love and desire — it is an image as old as love-poetry,
the stuff of many a pop song; but, as 'One Cigarette' shows,
Morgan can revivify it into fresh poetry. Like the other images
we have examined, it contains its own sad opposite. The satis-
faction of desire is happiness itself, but the bright flame will die

eventually, leaving only ashes. But especially in the sequence in *The Second Life*, where the image is most prominent, the emphasis is on how love transforms the world into brightness and fire.

> How often when I think of you the day grows bright!
> . . . .

> Your breast and thighs were blazing like the gorse.
> I covered your great fire in silence there.
> We let the day grow old along the grass.
>   ('From a City Balcony')

> No, there is no spirit standing in the sun,
> only a great light and heat, that instantly
> surround us when we meet.
>   ('The Witness')

> When love comes late, but fated,
> the very ground seems on fire with tongues of running time . . .
> ('The Welcome')

Fire's opposite also recurs — images of water employed just as they are in 'Glasgow Green' to suggest cleansing, fertility, life itself. This water imagery is confined to the poems in *The Second Life*, which are more optimistic in tone than the other sequences. Falling rain suggests the grey Glasgow settings, but much more often it is rain that falls on the parched earth bringing life to hidden roots of desire, rain that cleanses away frustration, rain as a symbol of life and love:

> In this Glasgow balcony who pours
> such joy like mountain water? It brims, it spills over and over
> down to the parched earth and the relentless wheels.
>   ('From a City Balcony')

> I let the darkening room
> drink up the evening, till
> rest, or the new rain
> lightly roused you awake.
> I asked if you heard the rain in your dream
> and half dreaming still you only said, I love you.
>   ('When You Go')

If all goodbyes could be drowned in one welcome,
and the pain of waiting be washed from a hundred street-corners,
and dry rebuffs and grey regrets, backs marching into rain
slip like a film from the soiled spirit made new —
I'd take that late gift, and those tongues
of fire would burn out in our
thankful fountains, to the sea.
  ('The Welcome')

The *From Glasgow to Saturn* sequence, in which the themes of distrust and separation are reflected in images of cold and darkness, is much darker in tone than the love poems in *The Second Life*.

Isolating and classifying images from different poems in the way illustrated above is rather like tearing up flowers from their proper and natural places in a garden. It is necessary for the purposes of analysis, but we should remember that the image truly lives only in the context of the complete poem or sequence of poems. Regarded as a unit, Morgan's love-poetry makes up one of his most appealing achievements. It strikes a personal note we do not often find elsewhere and, at the same time, it is truly universal, employing an imagery of earth, water and fire which is both simple and powerful.

VOICES

No-one can read Edwin Morgan's poetry without being struck by the fact that a very great deal of it is written in the first person singular. Usually, when poets write in the first person, they are conveying their own experience, emotions and opinions. Morgan does this of course, for example, in his love-poetry, but equally as often he uses the first person to give not himself, but the rest of the world, a voice. As he has pointed out in an interview — 'I think a lot of my poetry is in either a straight or some disguised form of dramatic monologue, and I quite often do try to give an animal a voice, just as I might give an object a voice as in 'The Apple's Song', just to get everything speaking, as it were . . . I feel that the whole world is able to express something'.[5]

Morgan's practice more than lives up to his announced intention. He has given 'voices' to a remarkable and unlikely variety of both living creatures and inanimate objects: for example, a hyena, a space module, Mount Caucasus, Edith Piaf, St Columba, Kierkegaard, Lord Jim, the Loch Ness Monster, an Egyptian mummy, men from the planet Mercury, trees, Vico, Sir Henry Morgan, a shadow, an archaeopteryx, a pair of cats, Eve, Grendel and Jack London.[6] An astonishing list! (See note at the end of the booklet). Morgan's desire to 'get everything' (and everyone) speaking has been a feature of his poetry right from the beginning. It is demonstrated also by his early (and continued) interest in translation, giving foreign literature a 'voice' in English.

The second major collection, *From Glasgow to Saturn*, is particularly notable for its profusion of first-person verse. Many of the poems include the word 'song' in their titles — for example, 'Columba's Song', 'Kierkegaard's Song', 'The Apple's Song', 'Song of the Child', 'The Loch Ness Monster's Song'. All of these poems are written in the first person.

Morgan has also mentioned his liking for the dramatic monologue form. A dramatic monologue is a poem which consists of the words of a single character (or sometimes an object with Morgan) who reveals in his speech his own nature and the dramatic situation in which he is involved. This is similar to a speech from a play made by one character, but there is an important difference: a dramatic monologue is complete and separate from anything else, while a speech in a play is only a part of a larger whole.

A good example of a dramatic monologue from Morgan's work is 'Good Friday' in which a Glasgow man who is drunk on a bus talks to an 'educated' man (presumably the poet) about the meaning of Easter. A frame is provided by his entrance and exit, which are very briefly described at the beginning and end of the poem respectively. But the bulk of the poem consists of his monologue addressed to his silent fellow-passenger. The monologue demonstrates Morgan's marvellous ear for speech. The speaker is rambling, incoherent and repetitive, but terribly friendly and anxious to communicate:

> I've had a wee drink, ye understand —
>   . . .   I don't say it's right
> I'm no saying it's right, ye understand — ye understand?
>   . . .   see what I mean?
>   . . .   know what I mean
> he's jist bliddy ignorant — Christ aye,
> bliddy ignorant. Well —

Dramatic monologue often has malicious intent; the object of the writer to have the speaker condemn himself out of his own mouth, as in Browning's 'My Last Duchess' or Burns's 'Holy Willie's Prayer'. There is very little of this in Morgan's poem. There is, instead, an amused tolerance implied for the friendly feckless soul in the bus. He is ignorant, but he admits his ignorance. He is the worse for drink, but that too is admitted. His intentions, 'to get some Easter eggs for the kiddies', are or were of the best. A kindly concern for his listener's welfare is manifest — 'I'm no boring you, eh?'

Like 'Trio', the poem contains irony, and it is a gentle irony. Morgan is making no great point concerning the speaker's insecure grasp of the meaning of Easter. To do so would be employing a sledgehammer to crack a walnut. The lines

> I don't know what today's in aid of,
> whether Christ was — crucified or was he —
> rose fae the dead like, see what I mean?

inevitably remind us of this from 'Trio':

> Whether Christ is born, or is not born, you
> put paid to fate . . .

In both poems the vibrant life of the here and now is sufficient in itself.

Other ironical touches occur. For example, we are told it is
'three o'clock', the traditional hour of Christ's crucifixion. The
blasphemy, 'Christ aye', is as much amusingly ironical as blas-
phemous in its context.

The narrative frame at the beginning and end of the poem is
deftly expressive. The bus 'lurches' round a corner — a prefigur-
ation of the drunk man, perhaps — and the man himself 'flops'
into his seat. When leaving, he 'lunges' for the stair and then
lay-out wittily suggests meaning as he goes off:

> on very
>   nearly
>   steady
>   legs.

A natural extension of an interest in monologue is to explore a theme through several voices rather than one, and this
we duly find in Morgan. Sometimes he uses a series of linked
monologues as in 'Stobhill' (from *From Glasgow to Saturn*) and
'Ten Theatre Poems' (from *The New Divan*). Monologue is by
definition 'insulated': the character speaks without interruption,
explaining and justifying to an unheard presence. Presumably
the speaker in monologue is trying to communicate, but the
question of whether he is actually communicating with the
unheard presence does not really arise. Dialogue on the other
hand — speech between two or more characters — implies
communication immediately. It is hard to carry on a conversation if there is no communication.

Morgan is evidently interested in this crucial difference between monologue and dialogue, because throughout his work
we find many dialogues. Moreover, these dialogues tend to high-
light the communication issue which has just been explained,
because they almost always involve speakers who are so very
different in culture or language that communication would
seem, on the face of it, impossible. For example, in 'The First
Men on Mercury', explorers from earth meet the inhabitants of
Mercury and the conversation begins as follows:

> — We come in peace from the third planet.
> Would you take us to your leader?
>
> — Bawr stretter! Bawr. Bawr. Stretterhawl?
>
> — This is a little plastic model
> of the solar system, with working parts.

You are here and we are there and we
are now here with you, is this clear?

— Gawl horrop. Bawr. Abawrhannahanna!

A study of the whole poem will reveal that the communication
theme develops in an unexpected and amusing way. Other
poems in similar vein include 'The Barrow: a dialogue', 'Boxers',
'Interview' and 'The Mummy'.

After these general considerations it will be useful to examine some illustrative poems. Morgan has spoken of trying 'to
give an animal a voice'. A good example of this is the poem '
'Hyena' from the collection *From Glasgow to Saturn*. In the
poem Morgan gives us the words of an African hyena. The
hyena addresses us directly in a series of statements and questions which create the menace of a creature which waits to feed
on carrion, a creature which inspires both disgust and fear in
human beings:

I am waiting for you.
I have been travelling all morning through the bush
and not eaten.
I am lying at the edge of the bush
on a dusty path that leads from the burnt-out kraal.

Notice the repetition of 'I am'. This takes place throughout
the poem, creating the effect of a creature toally absorbed in its
own necessary being. The sense of menace is increased by a
series of insinuating questions which suggest a villainous, ingrat-
iating craftiness:

What do you think of me? ...

Do you like my song? ...

Oh and my tongue — do you like me
when it comes lolling out over my jaw
very long, and I am laughing?

But the questions have a teasing quality also. The hyena is not
really interested in human reactions which are in any case mis-
taken:

I am not laughing.
But I am not snarling either, only
panting in the sun, showing you

> what I grip
> carrion with.

The last verse returns to the first line:'I am waiting?' The hyena almost functions as a mememto mori, a reminder of death, because it is waiting for dead flesh, waiting 'till you are ready for me'. In its presentation of the hyena, the poem invites an interesting comparison with Ted Hughes's well-known poem 'Hawk Roosting'.

A very different poem, at least in tone — one which gives an object a voice — is 'The Apple's Song'. Where the hyena's voice is self-absorbed, insinuating, menacing, the apple's voice is cheerful, friendly, outgoing. The poem is full of verbs and, because the stresses fall on these verbs, a lively rhythm is created at the beginning:

> Tap me with your finger,
> rub me with your sleeve,
> hold me, sniff me, peel me
> curling round and round
> till I burst out white and cold
> from my tight red coat
> and tingle in your palm ...

The 't' sounds from lines 5 to 7 reflect the sense of these lines — the neat precise coat of the apple restraining the tasty interior. Above all, the apple wants to be eaten! And this wish of the apple — to be eaten — exemplifies an important point about Morgan's attempts 'to get everything speaking'. Although he is, to an extent, personifying the apple, giving it a human voice and consciousness, he is determined to avoid any suggestion that an apple's emotional make-up is similar to a human being's emotional make-up. When Morgan personifies a creature or an object, he does so only to the degree that he gives it a voice; he does not endow it with conventional human emotions or reactions. On the contrary, he is concerned to show the strangeness, the 'otherness', the non-human nature of the creature or object. To this end language is often changed or manipulated, even twisted and distorted.

In 'Thoughts of a Module' a space-module sits on the surface of the moon 'thinking' and reacting to the experience. As so often, Morgan is forcing the reader to approach a subject from a totally new perspective. We are fairly used to the human perspective, the human reaction to space travel, but suppose a machine had thoughts on the matter:

It is black so. There is that dust.
My ladder is light. What are my men.
One is foot down. That is pack drill.
Black what is vizor. A hiss I heard.
The talks go up. Clump now but float.
Is a jump near. A camera paced out ...

The thoughts consist of a series of very short statements and
questions, two per line. The order of the words is consistently
strange; the questions seem odd, not based on any human logic;
the connections between the thoughts seem arbitrary. It is possible to rearrange some (but not all) of the sentences and make
sense of them, but it would be a pointless exercise: the whole
effect of the poem is dependent on the strangeness of the language and the sound of the strangeness. The complete poem,
however, conveys a clear powerful sense of what it must be like
to be on the surface of the moon.

So far we have considered single monologues, but Morgan
has also occasionally used a series of monologues to explore a
theme in depth. An outstanding example is the poem 'Stobhill'
from *From Glasgow to Saturn*. Like so many of Morgan's
poems, it is based on an event which was widely reported in the
press: an aborted foetus, which was taken to a hospital inciner-
ator for disposal, was discovered by the boilerman to be alive.
The resulting scandal led to a public enquiry. Morgan explores
the issues involved in a series of monologues delivered by the
principal characters involved: the doctor who performed the
operation; the boilerman who discovered that the supposedly
dead foetus was a living baby; the mother; the father; and finally the hospital porter who took the baby in a plastic bag to
the boilerman. These monologues are wonderfully varied, illuminating both characters and the wider social issues raised by the
event. No poem of Morgan's demonstrates his mastery of monologue with more assurance. It is highly recommended for close
study.

SPACE

In November 1957 a crucial event in the history of space exploration took place: the Soviet Union successfully launched its second earth satellite, Sputnik II. Morgan described his reactions in a poem called 'The Unspoken':

When the television newscaster said
the second sputnik was up, not empty
but with a small dog on board,
a half-ton treasury of life orbiting a thousand miles above the
    thin television masts and mists of November,
in clear space, heard, observed,
the faint far heartbeat sending back its message
steady and delicate,
and I was stirred by a deep confusion of feelings,
got up, stood with my back to the wall and my palms pressed
    hard against it, my arms held wide
as if I could spring from this earth
not loath myself to go out that very day where Laika had
    shown man,
felt my cheeks burning with old Promethean warmth
rekindled — ready —
covered my face with my hands, seeing only an animal
strapped in a doomed capsule, but the future
was still there, cool and whole like the moon,
waiting to be taken, smiling even
as the dog's bones and the elaborate casket of aluminium
glow white and fuse in the arc of re-entry,
and I knew what I felt was history,
its thrilling brilliance came down,
came down,
comes down on us all, bringing pride and pity.

Poets have often shied away from the worlds of industry, science, technology and space-exploration; seeing these, perhaps, as impersonal threats to the integrity and welfare of the human individual. Morgan, however, has never shared these fears and in this poem he positively thrills to human history in the making; the first earth-life in space, the little dog, Laika. 'Pity' for the fate of the dog when the satellite burns upon re-entry to the earth's atmosphere is more than balanced by 'pride'

and the 'thrilling brilliance' of history being made. The future is
'waiting to be taken'.

'The Unspoken' is, in fact, a love-poem, but the middle
verse quoted above shows all the typical elements of Morgan's
later 'space' poetry. First of all there is the excitement of the
exploration of new worlds. A journey is often involved, in space
and time. This journey usually requires change, readjustment,
for those taking part in it and the change is a change in emotional
attitudes, because Morgan's space poems are not celebrations of
cold technology. Quite the opposite. The mixture of emotions
engendered towards the little dog, Laika, at once a pathetic
doomed prisoner in its capsule and simultaneously the repository of human history and pride in achievement, is typical of
Morgan's attitude.

The space poems also make use of fairly common science-
fiction concepts: encounters between humans and alien beings;
journeys back and forward in time as well as space; the abandon-
ment of a doomed earth at some point in the future. The poem
'In Sobieski's Shield' deals with the latter situation. Earth has
been destroyed by 'solar withdrawal', but one family has es-
caped by 'dematerialisation' to a new life 'on a minor planet of
a sun in Sobieski's Shield'. The father describes the experience
in unrhymed unpunctuated verse which reflects the uncertainty
of their new situation. First of all, there is relief that they have
'made it' relatively intact, but with Morgan space journeys involve change. The father observes that he has only four fingers
on his left hand and that his son has only one nipple. Minor,
even humorous inconveniences, it seems, but there are deeper,
more significant changes. His wife has acquired a:

> strange and beautiful crown of
>   bright red hair.

His son's voice has broken during the process of de- and re-
materialisation:

> at thirteen he is a man
> what a limbo to lose childhood in

The most curious change, however, has taken place in the narr-
ator, the father, who notices a sort of birth mark which has
mysteriously appeared on his right fore-arm in the shape of a
heart:

> and one most curious
> I almost said birthmark and so it is in a sense

> light brown shaped like a crazy heart spreading
> across my right forearm well let it be . . .

Later the father sees a vision of 'the great war was it called
France Flanders field I remember'. Above the mud sticks the
arm of a dead soldier; on the arm a tattoo of a heart identical to
the mysterious mark on his own arm. The family have carried a
part of their human history with them to their harsh new home:

> . . . I have
> a graft of war and ancient agony.

They are still children of earth. The father knows that:

> . . . these flashes will return
> from the far past times I gather my wife and son to me
> with a fierce gesture that surprises them I am not
> a demonstrative man yet how to tell them
> what and who I am that we are bound to all that lived
> though the barriers are unspeakable.

Throughout the poem, and again in the final lines, the phrase
'the second life' occurs. Their second life will be very different
from their first on their new inhospitable home of metallic plains
and mineral storms, but they carry their human heritage with
them. 'It's hard to go let's go' says the father leading them out
from the dome. The poem is reminiscent of Arthur Clarke's
'2001: A Space Odyssey'. In it we see the typical elements of
Morgan's approach: space, a journey, a return, the tattoo as a
moving symbol of humanity (like the little dog in 'The Unspoken') and above all the final optimistic confrontation of the
future.

Morgan does not confine himself to the theme of humanity
exploring space and reacting to the experience. Sometimes he
reverses the process and describes how other beings react to their
encounters with humanity. In 'From the Domain of Arnheim',
beings from another planet use time travel to observe mankind
at an early stage of development — when he was living in caves.
The poem is strangely moving because it is our ancestors who
are being described — naked, primitive, but profoundly human:

> They sang naked, and kissed in the smoke.
> A child, or one of their animals, was crying.

The time travellers from outer space realize that they have come
upon a celebration for the birth of a baby:

> The crying
> came from one just born: that was the cause
> of the song. We saw it now. What had we stopped
> but joy?

The aliens can only observe, they cannot change anything, but their presence is sensed by the cave people:

> Yet they sensed us, stopped, looked up — even into our eyes.
> To them we were a displacement of the air,
> a sudden chill, yet we had no power
> over their fear.

The primitive men are afraid, but they are prepared to fight the strange alien presences amongst them. One of them seizes a brand from the fire and flings it:

> where our bodies would have been —
> we felt nothing but his courage.

The poem is a splendid example of how Morgan can use a science-fiction theme to expand our consciousness and to confound our expectations. The visit to earth of arrogant and superior aliens who wish to subjugate mere 'earthlings' is a science-fiction cliché. This poem reverses that scenario. Our primitive ancestors emerge as impressive, even heroic. The time travellers go back to their own planet with food for thought. They have their mineral and biological samples, but more importantly they have a memory of the integrity and courage of humanity:

> We signalled to the ship; got back;
> our lives and days returned to us, but
> haunted by deeper souvenirs than any rocks or seeds.
> From time the souvenirs are deeds.

Morgan returns to this theme in the major poem 'Memories of Earth' from *The New Divan*. It is interesting to compare it with 'From the Domain of Arnheim'. Once again Morgan takes a science-fiction cliché — miniaturisation of beings so that they can undertake a dangerous journey — and revivifies it by imaginative and original treatment. Once again aliens are profoundly changed by contact with humanity.

Poems inspired by space or science-fiction occur in all of Morgan's major collections. In addition to those discussed above, it is worth reading 'For the International Poetry Incarnation' and 'Islands' from *The Second Life*. These two poems are expressions of Morgan's sheer enthusiasm for space exploration and are reminiscent of 'The Unspoken' which was discussed at the beginning of this chapter. *From Glasgow to Saturn* contains an interesting group in which science-fiction themes are combined with language experiments: 'Thoughts of a Module', 'The First Men on Mercury' and 'Spacepoem 3: Off Course'. The short collection *Star Gate*, published in 1979, consists entirely of science-fiction poems. These are difficult poems but they use the basic elements identified in this chapter: the original use of well-known science-fiction ideas, journeys, changes, the impact of aliens on humanity and of humanity on aliens.

EXPERIMENTAL

The title of this chapter is rather misleading, because the word 'experimental' might be taken to imply tentative trials rather than solid successes; the poet doodling away at this and that. The opposite is the case. Morgan is obviously as serious in his pursuit of new poetic forms as he is in his pursuit of the new in subject-matter. Moreover, he has succeeded, in the opinion of many competent judges, in widening the possibilities of poetry.

It is impossible in a booklet of this length to do anything like justice to the sheer range of Morgan's concrete and other experimental poetry. For one thing, some of his work such as 'Bestiary' (1968), 'Proverbfolder' (1969) and 'Colour Poems' (1978) requires colour reproduction. What follows is an analysis of the poetry which depends on lay-out, on typographical reproduction.

The outstanding example of Morgan's interest in the innovative and experimental is his work in the field of concrete poetry, examples of which are to be found in all his major collections. Concrete poetry developed in Brazil in the 1950s and 60s. Important exponents were Haroldo de Campos and Eugen Gomringer. This is a poetry which moves away as far as possible from the traditional idea of the poem as a sequence of words in lines which conveys meaning to the reader. The emphasis, instead, is on the poem as an object on the page, an object for the reader to look at rather than read. Meaning is conveyed by shape and typographical arrangement rather than by words. Here is an example by Morgan called 'Siesta of a Hungarian Snake':

s sz sz SZ sz SZ sz ZS zs ZS zs zs z

That is the complete poem. The clue, the sign-post for the reader, as so often in concrete poetry, lies in the title. The poem shows first the shape of the snake stretched out on the ground. Perhaps it is thicker in the middle because it has just eaten and is sleeping off its meal. The 'sz' lettering is a traditional means of indicating sleep in comics and cartoons, but it also suggests visually the pattern of markings on the snake. Why a 'Hungarian' snake? In the Hungarian language, 'sz' and 'zs' are frequent letter combinations.

This analysis, which is based largely on Morgan's own comments, demonstrates how concrete poetry can, at its best, make a number of points entertainingly and economically if we look (rather than read) with an open mind.

Morgan began experimenting with concrete poetry during the sixties. The short collections, *Emergent Poems* (1967), *Gnomes* (1968) and *The Horseman's Word* (1970) consist entirely of innovative poetry, while concrete poetry is the largest single category in the major collection, *The Second Life* (1968). Thereafter the number of concrete poems falls off, although they occur right through to *The New Divan* (1977). It is possible to arrange his concrete poetry, tentatively, into several distinct types.

The first type might be termed 'pure' concrete poetry. These are poems in which the shape on the page, the typographical arrangement, is a crucial element. 'Siesta of a Hungarian Snake', already discussed, is such a poem. Others are 'The Chaffinch Map of Scotland' and 'Construction for I. K. Brunel', both from *The Second Life.*

'The Chaffinch Map of Scotland' is a particularly delightful and witty concrete poem. The poem consists of the various Scottish dialect words for the chaffinch typographically arranged to form the geographical shape of Scotland. Each dialect word is, of course, in its appropriate location in the 'map' thus formed. The result is clever, informative and, when read, also a subtle blend of sounds, because the dialect words are mostly variants on a single original word. 'Construction for I. K. Brunel' plays imaginatively both with the letters of Brunel's name and the great engineering achievements that made him famous, all within a shape that suggests a work of engineering.

The second type of concrete poetry consists of poems in which variations are rung upon a theme by repeating, rearranging and slightly changing certain basic words or phrases. The poet plays with language; sometimes with serious intent, sometimes for fun, sometimes both. 'Centaur', already analysed, belongs to this category. This is a poetry of sound as well as sense, which should be read in a linear fashion from beginning to end, as well as being looked at as a structure on the page. A typical example is 'Astrodome' which was inspired (like so many of Morgan's poems) by a news item: 'As real grass withers in the Astrodome at Houston, Texas, it has been replaced by Astrograss'. Here is the poem:

all is not grass that astrograss
that astrograss is not all grass
that grass is not all astrograss
astrograss is not all that grass
is that astrograss not all glass
not all astrograss is that glass
all that glass is not astrograss
that is not all astrograss glass
that glass is not all fibreglass
not all that fibreglass is glass
fibreglass is not all that glass
is that not all fibreglass glass
that fibreglass is not all grass
glass is not all that fibreglass
is all astrograss not that glass
all is not grass that fibregrass

Many readers, confronted by what seems such senseless repetition, shy away impatiently, but the clue, surely, is in the
original news items. Morgan was obviously struck by the totally
man-made nature of this exciting new structure, the astrodome.
The poem seems to reflect, almost, a struggle between the real
and the artificial. Hence the variations between 'grass', 'astrograss', 'glass' and fibreglass'. However, the poem ends with the
new word, 'fibregrass', suggesting that change, development, is
the essence of our modern age. Similar poems in which sound,
word-arrangement. repetition and word-variation are all central
include 'Pomander', 'Bees' Nest', and 'The Computer's First
Christmas Card'. These poems exhibit also the struggle towards
a final outcome which is noticeable in 'Astrodome'. 'The Computer's First Christmas Card' is particularly recommended as an
amusing example for further study.
      In a third type of concrete poem Morgan uses the technique
of subtracting words or letters from a base statement. The base
statement is usually a well-known quotation from literature or
history. Different words or letters are subtracted in each line.
The result is given point by the emergence of relevant words
from what remains of the base statement, words which form the
poem. A good example is 'Manifesto' from the significantly-
named *Emergent Poems:*

```
r      i  se
                 st an    d
pro        v e
                 st a        y
      t r                    y
    r  et r                  y
    le ar          n
          r    e   a     d
          t r      a     in
               s   tra   in
               v         i    ●
    le a               d
         t    e   st
    r  et     c   ət
    pro  t    e   st
    ro   a        r
    p      r    e   s              s
    p      ri       s              e
    pr     i         n             t
      e                  di        t
               s   a         y
    proletari      an s   in
        e    v e   r         y
        1          an    d
          a        r             e
          o        n             e
```

proletarii vsekh stran soedinyaites

The base statement is the famous closing sentence of the 'Communist Manifesto' written by Marx and Engels in 1847: 'proletarii vsekh stran soedinyaites' which is usually translated into English as 'Workers of the world, unite!' By using the subtraction technique, Morgan has created a poem which conveys the spirit of the communist struggle. The base statement takes on a new significance as the repository in another language of that spirit.

'Message Clear', which uses the biblical 'I am the resurrection and the life' is another poem that demonstrates this technique interestingly. Finally, here is part of 'French Persian Cats Having a Ball':

```
chat
shah    shah
        chat
                chat    shah    cha    ha
                shah    chat    cha    ha
        shah
        chat
cha
cha
```

It is possible to come to terms with this clever poem and others, by following some simple hints: look for clues in the title; consider the shape of the poem and the typographical arrangement; note the use of repetition and word variation and how the poet is playing with language. Morgan's experimental poetry is often a lot of fun, for the poet and then for the reader — if it is approached with an open mind.

THE NEW DIVAN

'The New Divan' is the title-poem of Morgan's third major collection. It is probably his most complex and difficult creation, but it is also, in the opinion of many critics including the present writer, his most satisfying achievement to date. All that can be offered here are some general hints about how 'The New Divan' should be approached by the reader, because a detailed analysis is beyond the scope of this booklet.

First of all, the description 'poem' is probably a misnomer in the case of 'The New Divan', certainly for the reader coming to it for the first time, and any attempt to read it from beginning to end as a completely structured poem will only lead to confusion and frustration. In fact, it consists of a hundred short poems, which are numbered but untitled. These hundred poems have various inter-connections and features in common, but essentially 'The New Divan' is a loosely-structured sequence of poems which should be approached in a flexible open-minded way. Some of them will be appreciated and understood fairly readily, while others will present difficulties. The reader has to build gradually towards an understanding of the complete sequence.

Any attempt to state, in a simple and straightforward way, what 'The New Divan' is 'about' is fraught with the same difficulties encountered when attempting to read it as a structured poem. It is about many things — the relationship between past and present, history, love, war, death, archaeology, man's place in the universe, Morgan's own experience. It is about man's life in the world and the last line of poem 53 (a quotation from the modern Austrian philosopher, Ludwig Wittgenstein) might well serve as a tentative summary of the subject-matter of the whole sequence

the world is everything that is the case

After these rather discouraging remarks, there is some good news. 'The New Divan', for all its difficulties, is an immensely enjoyable reading experience and there does exist a key that can take us into the world of the sequence. That key is 'setting'. The setting is the Middle East and the simplest, most flexible way to read the poems is as an evocation of various aspects of the Middle Eastern world and its history. Much of the enjoyment

comes from the rich mouth-filling language Morgan employs to
create this setting:

> Lamb sizzling, coffee like honeyed tar, raspberry-loads
> rolling like Brobdingnagian caviar — the way of
> the thing was all prodigal, in the direction
> of crashing sunsets and a bay of sails, over old
> cries of water-sellers, with a flick
> of the lamp the veranda
> could be swarming with jinn
>   (Poem 91)

The sequence is packed with vivid pictures, many of them based
on Morgan's own experience in the Middle East during World
War II. Here, for example, is poem 89, a description of one of
the legendary Egyptian belly-dancers, performing for an audience of British soldiers:

> She had nipple spangles and a tam-o-shanter.
> She was big and brown. Her legs were covered
> by some shanghaied sailor's half-split fall-fronts. About
> midnight was her spot. Her kind of men,
> shining with beer like children, could do without
> seven veils. 'Oh get in
> there,' they roared when she crossed the stage.
> Her nostrils flared as she got scent of
> that Port Said music. A tremor, unrehearsed,
> made ancient grossness regal. Socks,
> stardust, headgear came off. Guarded
> by a lattice of trouser-cloth her belly-dance struck.
> Whistles and piastres seemed theatrical
> as she stood and shook out sin and dross and drowsiness.

It is possible to recognise short groups of poems within the
sequence. Poems 32 to 35, for instance, evoke the discomfort of
an archaeological excavation in the Arabian desert. The ferocity
of the noonday sun has seldom been better described than this:

> Bounced glaring through the awnings,
> a sun with the strength of ten
> curdled milk and frayed men.
> This was the noon of the Arabians.
> We filled notebooks, eyed the waterskins.

> Weighing fossils kept thirst
> at bay until chat trailed off and
> wondering what the ammonites had drunk
> we took a sip and fell asleep.
>   (Poem 34)

Finding these short groups within the sequence and coming to terms with them enables the reader to build up an understanding of the whole sequence.

The word 'divan' has various meanings which Morgan uses in the sequence. First of all, it signifies a collection of poems. The greatest of Persian lyric poets, Hafiz (1326-1390), collected his five hundred poems on life and love into his 'Divan'. Morgan does the same in 'The New Divan'. Hafiz is sometimes addressed directly by Morgan, specifically in the opening and closing poems. In one respect Morgan's sequence is a tribute to his fellow poet. 'Divan', however, also means an Oriental council of state which sits in judgement on difficult problems. This illuminates another aspect of 'The New Divan', because the sequence is highly philosophical. Morgan speculates on the great human questions — the meaning of life, the significance of history, the finality or otherwise of death.

In the wider context of his work, 'The New Divan' is a truly new and impressive achievement, because, as we have seen, Morgan is very much a poet of present experience and future possibilities. He instinctively distrusts the past, the backward glance, aware always of the dangers of nostalgia and sentimentality. However, in 'The New Divan' he explores the past, both his personal past and the historical past of the Middle East, with subtlety and insight. Most wonderfully of all, the free verse paragraph, a form which Morgan has been mastering over three decades, has become in these poems a pliant sensuous medium which Morgan varies according to the demands of his material. In the final poem he gives us a final clue to what he has been about — he has been speaking of 'memories crowding in':

> The dead climb with us like the living to the edge.
> The clouds sail and the air's washed blue. For you
> and me, the life beyond the sages mention
> is this life on a crag above
> a line of breakers. Oh I can't speak
> of that eternal break of white, only of
> memories crowding in from human kind,
> stealthily, brazenly, thankfully, stonily

into that other sea-cave
of my head. Down where the breaker was
closes, darkens, rises, foams, closes; crates
drift across, whirl round
in the ghost of a gale;
a shred of sailcloth
relic of a gale
that really blew slews to the resting-place
the long tide goes out
to leave it, bleaching on its bony rock.
I pick it from the stone,
Hafiz, to bind the leaves of my divan.

CONCLUSION

Tracing Morgan's development as a poet is a task to be approached with some caution. As should be clear by now, he is a poet who has always resisted easy categorisation, whether by technique or by subject-matter. Many poets employ the same techniques, explore the same subject-matter, throughout their work. Tracing their development is usually a matter, therefore, of evaluating success or failure in simple comparative terms: 'this poem is better than that poem on the same subject because . . . ' With good writers, of course, technique tends to become more skilful and assured, the exploration deeper and more complex, with experience

Morgan's case is not so simple because so often he tries new things; new techniques, new forms, new subject-matter which do not offer the opportunity for simple comparisons. The 'shock of the new' has often meant with Morgan that judgements have had to be tentative or suspended: 'this is very interesting, but I'm not quite sure what to make of it . . . ' The reader or critic is forced to rely on analysis alone rather than the twin critical techniques of analysis and comparison.

In his most recent publications (up to 1985), Edwin Morgan has continued to demonstrate his capacity for new invention. Since 'The New Divan' his most significant work has been *Sonnets from Scotland* (Mariscat, 1984). In this he uses the traditional sonnet form in a variety of exciting new ways to range over the topic of Scotland past, present and future. As a conclusion to the study of Morgan's poetry in this booklet, Appendix I presents one of these sonnets for practical criticism so that the student may do a personal analysis of a poem by Morgan with a few guiding questions to focus the thinking.

NOTES

1   From Morgan's introduction to the selection of his work in *Worlds*
     (Penguin Education, 1974).
2   From *Rites of Passage*, p. 45.
3   From Morgan's introduction to *Sovpoems* (Migrant Press, 1961).
4   From *Worlds* (Penguin Education, 1974).
5   From *Edwin Morgan: an interview*, Marshall Walker (Akros, 1977),
     one of the most helpful publications on Morgan. The poet speaks
     frankly and illuminatingly on his poetry and his ideas about poetry.
6   Notes on people/creatures mentioned in this paragraph.

Mount Caucasus: a famous mountain near the Caspian Sea. In Greek
mythology Prometheus (generally considered as representative of
mankind's enterprising spirit) was tied to the peak of Caucasus by
Zeus and continually eaten by vultures. The key image of red in
Morgan's poem 'Mt. Caucasus' refers to this myth.

St Columba (521-97): Irish missionary who founded a monastery on
the Scottish island of Iona about 563. The conversion of the northern
Picts of Scotland is usually credited to him. 'Columba's Song' records
his initial reactions to the wild Scottish Highlands. Brude was the
King of the northern Picts.

Kierkegaard (1813-55): Danish philospher, forerunner of various
modern philosophers who distrust reason as a guide in human affairs.
Morgan's poem, 'Kierkegaard's Song', mirrors this by contrasting a
crow's lumbering indecision about whether to take flight with the
sure unthinking flight of the kingfisher.

Lord Jim: a fictional character from Joseph Conrad's novel of the
same name. The novel is set in the Far East, the locale of Morgan's
'Lord Jim's Ghost's Tiger Poem'.

Vico (1668-1744): Italian philosopher mainly known for his theory
that all human history is a series of repetitions of the same set pattern. The poem, 'Vico's Song', reflects this theory in its form and
use of repetition.

Archaeopteryx: oldest known (fossil) bird, a link between birds and
reptiles. In 'The Archaeopteryx's Song' the creature laments its half-
way status.

Grendel: monster in the Anglo-Saxon poem, *Beowulf*. It lives in a
lake by day and attacks humankind by night. Morgan's 'Grendel'
neatly reverses the original story by having the monster express its
disgust with typical human behaviour.

Jack London (1876-1916): American writer of adventure stories who
himself lived an equally adventurous life. 'Jack London in Heaven' is
essentially about the unquenchable spirit of adventure. It can be use-
fully compared with Tennyson's poem 'Ulysses'.

APPENDIX 1

PRACTICAL CRITICISM

The poem which follows is called 'Pilate at Fortingall', from
Sonnets from Scotland (Mariscat, 1984). Fortingall is a village in
Perthshire which persistent legend associates with Pontius Pilate.

A Latin harsh with Aramaicisms
poured from his lips incessantly; it made
no sense, for surely he was mad. The glade
of birches shamed his rags, in paroxysms
he stumbled, toga'd, furred, blear, brittle, grey.
They told us he sat here beneath the yew
even in downpours; ate dog-scraps. Crows flew
from prehistoric stone to stone all day.
'See him now'. He crawled to the cattle-trough
at dusk, jumbled the water till it sloshed
and spilled into the hoof-mush in blue strands,
slapped with useless despair each sodden cuff,
and washed his hands, and watched his hands, and washed
his hands, and watched his hands, and washed his hands.

1   What Biblical event is obliquely referred to in the poem?
     Quote the lines which suggest the event.
2   Show how water imagery is developed throughout the
     poem.
3   Comment on the use of 's' sounds in the poem.
4   Comment on Morgan's use of the sonnet form in this poem.
5   Discuss how Morgan suggests the cause and nature of Pil-
     ate's condition. What is the significance of 'surely' in line 3?
6   Bearing in mind what you have learned about Morgan's
     poetry, discuss how this poem is or is not 'typical' of his
     subjects and methods.

APPENDIX 2

INDEX OF POEMS DISCUSSED

All poems, except 'Pilate at Fortingall' are to be found in *Poems of Thirty Years* (Carcanet); those marked with an asterisk are also to be found in *Edwin Morgan: Selected Poems* (Carcanet). Bold type indicates poems treated in some detail.

APPENDIX 3
SELECT BIBLIOGRAPHY

Poetry
Selected Poems (Manchester: Carcanet, 1985)
Collected Poems (Manchester: Carcanet, 1990)
Hold Hands Among the Atoms (Glasgow: Mariscat, 1991)
Virtual and Other Realities (Manchester: Carcanet, 1997)
Demon (Glasgow:Mariscat, 1999)
* *New Selected Poems* (Manchester: Carcanet, 2000)

Translations
Collected Translations (Manchester: Carcanet, 1996)

Drama
Edmond Rostand's Cyrano de Bergerac (Manchester: Carcanet, 1992) [translation]
Christopher Marlowe's Doctor Faustus in a new version (Manchester: Carcanet, 1999)
Jean Racine's Phaedra: a Tragedy (Manchester: Carcanet, 2000) [translation]
A.D.: a trilogy on the life of Jesus Christ (Manchester: Carcanet, 2000)

Prose
Essays (Manchester: Carcanet, 1974)
Crossing the Border: Essays on Scottish Literature (Manchester: Carcanet, 1990)
Edwin Morgan: Nothing Not Giving Messages – reflections on his work and life Ed. Hamish Whyte (Edinburgh: Polygon, 1990)

Criticism
About Edwin Morgan Eds. Robert Crawford and Hamish Whyte (Edinburgh: Edinburgh University Press, 1990)

* Specially recommended for students

SCOTNOTES

Study guides to major Scottish writers and literary texts

Produced by the Schools and Further Education Committee
of the Association for Scottish Literary Studies

Series Editors
Lorna Borrowman Smith
Ronald Renton

Editorial Board
Ronald Renton, St Aloysius' College, Glasgow
(Convener, Schools and Further Education Committee, ASLS)
William Aitken, Stevenson College, Edinburgh
Jim Alison, HMI (retired)
Gerard Carruthers, University of Strathclyde
Alistair Chynoweth, The High School of Dundee
Dr Morna Fleming, Beath High School, Cowdenbeath
Professor Douglas Gifford, University of Glasgow
John Hodgart, Garnock Academy, Kilbirnie
Alan MacGillivray, University of Strathclyde
Dr James McGonigal, University of Glasgow
Rev Jan Mathieson, University of Edinburgh
Lorna Ramsay, Fairlie
Dr Kenneth Simpson, University of Strathclyde
Lorna Borrowman Smith, Wallace High School, Stirling

THE ASSOCIATION FOR SCOTTISH LITERARY STUDIES aims to promote the study, teaching and writing of Scottish literature, and to further the study of the languages of Scotland.

To these ends, the ASLS publishes works of Scottish literature; literary criticism and in-depth reviews of Scottish books in *Scottish Studies Review*; short articles, features and news in *ScotLit*; and scholarly studies of language in *Scottish Language*. It also publishes *New Writing Scotland*, an annual anthology of new poetry, drama and short fiction, in Scots, English and Gaelic. ASLS has also prepared a range of teaching materials covering Scottish language and literature for use in schools.

All the above publications are available in return for an annual subscription. Schools can receive teaching materials by joining ASLS at a special reduced rate. Enquiries should be sent to:

ASLS, c/o Department of Scottish History, 9 University Gardens, University of Glasgow, Glasgow G12 8QH.

Telephone/fax +44 (0)141 330 5309
e-mail d.jones@asls.org.uk
www.asls.org.uk